SEPTEMBER 11
THROUGH THE EYES OF
GEORGE W. BUSH

by Emily O'Keefe

Peachtree

Content Consultant
Chris Edelson, JD
Assistant Professor of Government
School of Public Affairs, American University

Core Library

An Imprint of Abdo Publishing
abdopublishing.com

abdopublishing.com

Published by Abdo Publishing, a division of ABDO, PO Box 398166, Minneapolis, Minnesota 55439. Copyright © 2016 by Abdo Consulting Group, Inc. International copyrights reserved in all countries. No part of this book may be reproduced in any form without written permission from the publisher. Core Library™ is a trademark and logo of Abdo Publishing.

Printed in the United States of America, North Mankato, Minnesota
092015
012016

Cover Photo: Doug Mills/AP Images
Interior Photos: Doug Mills/AP Images, 1, 4, 32; William Kratzke/AP Images, 7, 45; Reuters/Corbis, 9; Chris O'Meara/AP Images, 10; Red Line Editorial, 12, 18; Eric Draper/Us National A/SIPA/Newscom, 14; US National Archive/Flickr, 17; Owen D. B./Black Star/Newscom, 20; Beth A. Keiser/AP Images, 24; Reuters/Tami Chappell/Corbis, 26; PHC Johnny Bivera Notimex/Newscom, 28; Chris Corder UPI Photo Service/Newscom, 34; Brooks Kraft/Corbis, 36; Wali Sabawoon/NurPhoto/Sipa USA/Newscom, 40

Editor: Jon Westmark
Series Designer: Laura Polzin

Library of Congress Control Number: 2015945412

Cataloging-in-Publication Data
O'Keefe, Emily.
 September 11 through the eyes of George W. Bush / Emily O'Keefe.
   p. cm. -- (Presidential perspectives)
ISBN 978-1-68078-034-5 (lib. bdg.)
Includes bibliographical references and index.
1. September 11 Terrorist Attacks, 2001--Juvenile literature. 2. Bush, George W. (George Walker), 1946-- Juvenile literature.   3. Presidents--United States--Juvenile literature.   I. Title.
973.931--dc23

2015945412

CONTENTS

UNDER ATTACK

September 11, 2001, began as a normal day for President George W. Bush. He was visiting Sarasota, Florida, to discuss education programs. Bush woke early and took a four-mile (6.4-km) run with members of his security staff. Then he met with his chief of staff, Andrew Card, to discuss the day's schedule. The main event would be a visit to Emma E. Booker Elementary School. Bush planned to read with

President George W. Bush cools down after a predawn run in Sarasota, Florida, on September 11, 2001.

students and then give a speech about education. By 8:45 a.m., the president's motorcade was on its way to the school.

Rumors of a Crash

Once he arrived, Bush received alarming news. A plane had crashed into one of the towers of the World Trade Center in New York City. The North and South Towers of the World Trade Center were important financial buildings. The two towers were each approximately 1,360 feet (415 m) high. Nearly 35,000 people worked in the buildings.

Bush knew few details about the crash. He thought a tragic accident had occurred. Perhaps a pilot had made a mistake. The president asked members of his staff to find more information about what happened. Bush said they would discuss the crash after the school visit.

At 9:00 a.m., Bush entered a classroom at the elementary school. He greeted the students and the teacher. The children began to read a book to

United Airlines Flight 175 approaches the South Tower of the World Trade Center. The South Tower was the second building hit during the attack.

the president. Meanwhile, some members of Bush's administration rushed to find a television so they could watch what was happening in New York.

Attack on America

The president's advisers hooked up a television in an empty classroom. News reporters were discussing the airplane crash. The television showed smoke spewing from the North Tower of the World Trade Center. As the president's staff watched, a second plane approached the towers. It crashed into the South Tower and exploded, killing the passengers on board and trapping thousands of people above the point of impact.

Once the second plane hit, it became clear the crashes were not accidents. The two planes had struck right next to each other. Bush's advisers believed hijackers had taken control of the planes and used them as weapons.

If it were an attack, it would not be the first on the World Trade Center. In 1993 a group of terrorists blew up a bomb below the North Tower. They hoped the explosion would make both towers fall. The blast killed six people, but the towers did not fall.

Chief of Staff Card believed it was a similar attack. At 9:05 a.m., he hurried to the front of the classroom where the president was reading with students. "A second plane hit the second tower," he whispered into Bush's ear. "America is under attack."

Chief of Staff Card informs Bush that a second plane has hit the World Trade Center. Bush was leading a reading lesson with students at the time.

Addressing the Situation

Bush had to think quickly about what to do. He was upset but did not want to scare the children. He decided not to leave the classroom right away. Bush's press secretary, Ari Fleischer, held up a notepad with a message for Bush to see. The message said, in large letters, "Don't say anything yet." Fleischer wanted to talk about the best way to respond to the attacks.

Bush observes a moment of silence during a televised address from Emma E. Booker Elementary School on September 11, 2001.

Bush remained calm and continued talking to the students. After the reading lesson, Bush and his advisers rushed to find a place to talk. They concluded that terrorists had attacked the United States. But many other questions remained.

Bush knew Americans would be worried and confused. Millions of people had seen the second crash on live television. Bush picked up a notepad and began writing a speech. Camera crews at the school were ready to record his statement. The president told Americans the government was working to find the attackers.

Lost in the Air

After his speech, Bush traveled to Air Force One, the president's official plane. He was eager to return to Washington, DC. At the White House, he could meet with more officials and discuss what happened. But soon he learned that Washington might also be under attack. A third plane had crashed into the Pentagon in Arlington, Virginia, which is near Washington, DC. The building plays

The Plane Hijackings

Nineteen hijackers took control of US planes on September 11. They had prepared for the attack for years. The hijackers studied airplane and airport security. Some got pilot licenses. During the attack, they used knives and other weapons to frighten passengers. Then they took control of the planes. Though the hijackings were terrifying, passengers showed heroism. On United Airlines Flight 93, the hijackers had planned to crash into a building in Washington, DC. But some passengers had heard about the other attacks. They fought the hijackers. Their fighting forced the hijackers to crash in a field in Shanksville, Pennsylvania. The 40 people on board the plane died, but the crash did not harm others outside the plane.

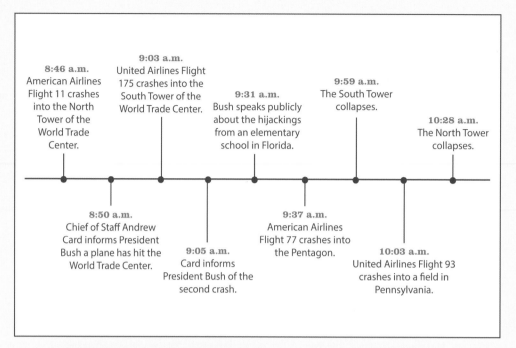

Timeline of September 11

This timeline lists the order of events on September 11. How does seeing the timeline help you think about the attacks differently?

an important role in managing the US military. There were reports that a fourth hijacked plane was heading toward Washington, DC.

Terrorists seemed to be targeting important US buildings. Some people feared the White House or the US Capitol could be next. Advisers told Bush to wait to return to Washington. Reluctantly, Bush agreed.

At 9:59 a.m., the South Tower of the World Trade Center collapsed from the damage caused by the airplane. The North Tower fell approximately half an hour later. Thousands of rescue workers had been near the buildings. At 10:03 a.m., the fourth hijacked plane crashed into a field in Pennsylvania.

Shortly before noon, the president's plane touched down at Barksdale Air Force Base in Louisiana. In a televised speech, Bush told Americans to be strong. "Freedom was attacked this morning," he declared. "And freedom will be defended."

EXPLORE ONLINE

Chapter One describes the four attacks that took place on September 11, 2001. The website below provides interactive maps of where the hijacked airplanes struck. How does seeing the maps help you better understand what occurred?

September 11 Interactive Maps
mycorelibrary.com/george-w.-bush

CHAPTER TWO

RESPONDING TO TERRORISM

George W. Bush had been president for only eight months. He was facing the greatest challenge of his time in office. In the afternoon of September 11, Bush held a videoconference with his leading advisers. George Tenet was the head of the Central Intelligence Agency (CIA). Bush asked Tenet who was responsible for the attack. Tenet responded, "Al-Qaeda."

President Bush arrives in Offutt Air Force Base in Nebraska on September 11, 2001. Bush held a videoconference with his advisers from the base.

President Bush had heard about al-Qaeda. They were a militant group that carried out terrorist acts. Members of al-Qaeda lived in many countries. Osama bin Laden was the leader of the group. No one knew exactly where bin Laden was. He and other al-Qaeda members kept their locations secret.

Al-Qaeda

Al-Qaeda is an Arabic term. It means "the base" or "the foundation." Members of al-Qaeda follow a very strict version of Islam that most Muslims reject. Members of al-Qaeda considered the September 11 attack to be an act of *jihad*, or "struggle." The term is sometimes translated as "holy war." Al-Qaeda members believed US policies were harming Muslims in the Middle East. In 1996 Osama bin Laden vowed to kill US citizens in revenge.

Coping with Disaster

That evening the president finally returned to the White House. There was much to be done. The government needed to help the people affected by the attacks. It also needed to find out who had committed the attacks. Bush addressed the nation again that

Bush, right, meets with Vice President Dick Cheney, left, and other senior staff members in the President's Emergency Operations Center beneath the White House.

evening. "None of us will ever forget this day, yet we go forward to defend freedom and all that is good and just in our world," he said.

World leaders expressed their support for the United States. Many offered to help catch the terrorists who planned the attack. Americans united in remembrance of the victims. Across the country, people held ceremonies. They honored those who

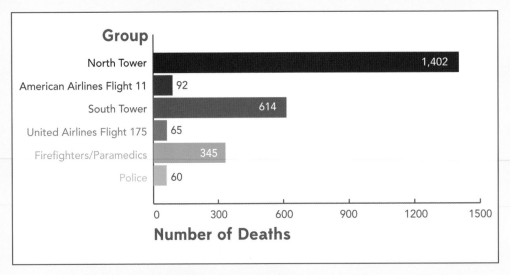

World Trade Center Deaths

Approximately 2,823 people died on September 11 in the World Trade Center attacks. Many were firefighters and police officers who responded to the attacks. The graph above shows the number of deaths that occurred due to the World Trade Center attack. How does it help you understand the September 11 attacks? What risks do you think firefighters faced?

died in the attacks. Many people put up flags to show their patriotism.

Meanwhile, New York in particular coped with the destruction. Fires continued to burn at the site of the fallen towers for days after the attack. The area, known as Ground Zero, was filled with debris. The destruction spanned ten city blocks. Police officers searched for survivors. Firefighters cleared rubble from the attack site. It was a long, difficult job. Breathing in chemicals from the smoke was dangerous. Some workers developed health problems.

On September 14, Bush visited Ground Zero. The workers inspired Bush. They showed heroism in the face of tragedy. Bush spoke to the city's mayor, Rudolph Giuliani. Police officers and firefighters waited to shake Bush's hand.

The president picked up a bullhorn. He began thanking the police officers and firefighters. One firefighter yelled that he could not hear the president. "I can hear you!" Bush shouted. "The rest of the world hears you! And the people who knocked these buildings down will hear all of us soon." The crowd cheered. Some chanted, "U-S-A!"

The president's visit raised people's spirits. It also made Bush more determined to find the people who had attacked the United States. This meant locating members of al-Qaeda.

Bush holds up the badge of a police officer who died in the World Trade Center attack during a speech in front of Congress on September 20, 2001.

Confronting Terror

Meanwhile, Congress easily passed a bill called the Authorization for Use of Military Force. Bush signed the bill into law on September 18. It allowed the president to use military action against those who planned the September 11 attacks and those who protected them.

On September 20, 2001, Bush gave a televised speech. He announced a national war on terrorism.

"Our war on terror begins with al-Qaeda, but it does not end there," he said. Bush's aim was not to punish only al-Qaeda. He believed other terrorist organizations could attack the United States. Bush announced the United States would not only fight terrorist groups. It would also fight countries that sheltered terrorists.

The president invited other nations to join in the war. The United Kingdom and Canada were long-time allies of the United States. These countries had helped Americans in the days after the September 11 attacks. Both nations were quick to pledge their support.

The United States had fought against other nations. But it had never gone to war against a group that did not represent a country. Bush needed to know how to find and eliminate the terrorists. The only way to defeat terrorism, he said, was to "destroy it where it grows."

In his speech on September 20, Bush announced the main location for the war on terror. Experts had evidence Osama bin Laden was living in Afghanistan. This country was also home to training camps for al-Qaeda members.

At the time, the Taliban ruled Afghanistan. This group believed in a harsh form of Islamic law. Their beliefs were often similar to al-Qaeda's. The Taliban did not officially support terrorism. But it was helping al-Qaeda leaders hide from the United States.

Bush demanded the Taliban give bin Laden to the United States. Bush also wanted the group to shut down al-Qaeda bases. But the Taliban refused.

September 11, 2002, was the one-year anniversary of the terrorist attacks. The following is an excerpt from the speech Bush gave to honor the victims:

> *The loss of so many lives left us to examine our own. Each of us was reminded that we are here only for a time, and these counted days should be filled with things that last and matter: love for our families, love for our neighbors, and for our country. . . . We resolved a year ago to honor every last person lost. We owe them remembrance, and we owe them more. We owe them, and their children, and our own, the most enduring monument we can build: a world of liberty and security made possible by the way America leads, and by the way Americans lead our lives.*

Source: George W. Bush. "Vigilance and Memory; Transcript of President Bush's Address to the Nation on Sept. 11 Anniversary." New York Times. The New York Times Company, September 12, 2002. Web. Accessed May 9, 2015.

What's the Big Idea?

Reread the passage carefully. What does Bush think people should learn from the attacks? Consider what Bush says about the United States. What might Bush identify as important US values?

CHAPTER THREE

AMERICA AT WAR

Confronting al-Qaeda in Afghanistan was an important part of the war against terrorism. President Bush wanted to protect the United States and bring those responsible for the September 11 attacks to justice. The president also needed to continue to support Americans dealing with the effects of the attacks.

Workers search for survivors in the rubble of the World Trade Center on September 13, 2001.

An airline ticket agent waits at an empty counter on September 13, 2001. Many Americans were afraid to fly following the September 11 attacks.

Safety at Home

On September 22, the president signed an act of Congress establishing the September 11 Victim Compensation Fund. This fund provided financial assistance to families of the victims.

Bush also took action to calm fears that more attacks would happen. On September 11, the Federal Aviation Administration had canceled thousands of commercial flights. It had also closed airports to prevent further attacks. Yet even after US airports reopened on September 13, many Americans were afraid to fly. Bush did not want Americans to suffer. He wanted them to get back to their normal routines.

On September 27, the president announced new air-safety measures. He called on 4,000 National Guard troops to protect airports. He said armed marshals would provide extra security on flights. Bush signed a bill into law giving money to airlines for new safety equipment. He believed video monitors could help crews identify problems quickly. And stronger cockpit doors could keep hijackers out.

Anthrax

In the weeks following September 11, another frightening new threat emerged in the United States, adding to public worry. US politicians and media outlets started to receive envelopes containing anthrax, a highly dangerous substance. The envelopes killed five people and sickened 17 more. The Federal Bureau of Investigation (FBI) investigated the anthrax attacks. Eventually the FBI concluded they were not connected to the hijackings. But at the time, the two threats seemed closely linked. Bush requested an increase in funds to prevent bioterrorism.

US marines travel to Afghanistan on December 18, 2001, during Operation Enduring Freedom.

Going to War

On October 7, 2001, US troops began bombing Afghanistan. That evening Bush gave a speech. He announced the beginning of Operation Enduring Freedom. This was the official name for the Afghanistan conflict.

Soon US ground troops arrived in Afghanistan. Bush also asked other nations for help. Several other countries formed a coalition with the United States. Canada and the United Kingdom sent military troops.

As war began in Afghanistan, Bush helped develop laws to identify possible terrorists in the United States. The new laws became known as the Patriot Act. The act set penalties for terrorist actions. It also gave the government new surveillance powers. This included access to records of Americans' phone calls, Internet history, and library use.

Bush believed the Patriot Act would help authorities discover connections between suspected terrorists. The government could then prevent planned attacks. Yet some people criticized the bill. They believed it targeted all Americans, not just terrorists. But the act easily passed through Congress. Most Americans supported the bill. On October 26, 2001, Bush signed the Patriot Act into law.

An Endless War?

In the first two months of the war in Afghanistan, coalition forces made significant progress. They removed the Taliban from power. A new government took control of the nation.

Opposing the Patriot Act

In 2001 most lawmakers voted to pass the Patriot Act. One person who voted against it was Wisconsin senator Russ Feingold. Feingold agreed the government should prevent terrorist attacks. But he thought the act limited Americans' privacy. The Patriot Act allowed the government to access Americans' personal information. Feingold believed this was not necessary to fight terrorism. In later years, lawmakers changed the law. On June 2, 2015, President Barack Obama signed the USA Freedom Act into law. The law put limits on what information the US government can collect about its citizens.

Yet the war was far from over. The new Afghan government struggled to keep control of the country. In December, Osama bin Laden escaped Afghanistan. Americans started to question the purpose of the war.

Bush encouraged Americans to stay hopeful. He ordered military actions in Pakistan and Somalia. Bush believed attacking terrorists abroad would protect Americans from another attack in the United States.

Bush believed terrorists were afraid of democracy. In September 2001, he discussed what he believed were al-Qaeda's reasons for attacking the United States. Bush spoke the following words in the US Capitol, where Congress meets:

> *Americans are asking, "Why do they hate us?" They hate what they see right here in this chamber: a democratically elected government. Their leaders are self-appointed. They hate our freedoms: our freedom of religion, our freedom of speech, our freedom to vote and assemble and disagree with each other.*
>
> *Source: George W. Bush. "Text: President Bush Addresses the Nation." Washingtonpost.com. Washington Post, September 20, 2001. Web. Accessed May 9, 2015.*

Point of View

Not everyone agrees that al-Qaeda attacked the United States because of its freedoms. Others say al-Qaeda attacked because of US policies. Does it matter why al-Qaeda attacked the United States? Why or why not?

A NEW ERA AT HOME

In the months following September 11, most Americans supported the president's response to the attacks. They admired his focus on national security. But Bush believed he could do more to protect the United States.

Homeland Security

Before September 11, several government agencies investigated terrorist attacks. These agencies included

Bush meets with his National Security Council on September 12, 2001. The National Security Council worked to plan the response to the September 11 attacks.

Bush signs the Homeland Security Act on November 25, 2002.

the CIA and the FBI. Sometimes the agencies did not share information with each other. For this reason, they could miss important clues.

On November 25, 2002, Bush signed the Homeland Security Act into law. The act was developed by members of Congress. It created the Department of Homeland Security. This department develops tools to combat terrorism and collaborates with other agencies.

One part of this department is the Transportation Security Administration (TSA). This agency is responsible for airport safety. In 2003 Bush directed government agencies to create a secret list. It contained the names of suspected terrorists. The TSA uses this tool, called the "no-fly list." People on the list are often prevented from boarding planes. Some Americans have criticized the list. It has contained mistakes. Because the list is secret, these mistakes are hard to correct.

Punishing Captured Terrorists

As Operation Enduring Freedom continued into 2003, the US government struggled to find information on Osama bin Laden's location. But agents captured other important al-Qaeda officials. Khalid Sheikh Mohammed had helped plan the September 11 attacks. On March 1, 2003, forces in Pakistan captured Mohammed. They turned him over to the United States. The government had to decide what to do with Mohammed and the other captured terrorists.

Guards escort a prisoner in Guantanamo Bay, Cuba, in 2002. The US army used the prison in Cuba to hold suspected terrorists.

The United States had a naval station in Guantanamo Bay, Cuba. Bush transformed it into a prison. The United States kept suspected terrorists there. People in the United States cannot be held unless they are charged with crimes. But Bush believed people suspected of terrorism should not be treated like other suspected criminals. Groups such as al-Qaeda had not signed treaties agreeing how prisoners should be treated during wartime.

By January 2002, the prison held 20 people. Two years later, 367 prisoners were held there. Khalid Sheikh Mohammed was among them. The prisoners could be kept as long as they were considered dangerous.

Some people believed the prison should be shut down. These critics believed everyone had the right to a trial. But most supported keeping prisoners at Guantanamo Bay rather than moving them to US prisons. They believed the prison in Cuba helped keep the United States safe.

Bush hoped investigators could get information from terror suspects that would help prevent

The Search for Osama bin Laden

During Bush's presidency, government agents searched for Osama bin Laden. But the search was long and difficult. It ended almost ten years after the September 11 attacks, long after Bush left office. American officials learned that bin Laden was hiding in Pakistan. A skilled team of navy commandos conducted a daring raid on his compound. On May 2, 2011, they found and killed bin Laden.

future attacks. The CIA tried many ways of getting information from prisoners at Guantanamo and other wartime prisons. Certain methods, such as waterboarding, were very harsh. Many people believe waterboarding is a form of torture. They say it is not an effective way to get information. But Bush stood by the use of waterboarding. He said it and other techniques helped get information that saved American lives.

Leaving Office

No other major attacks happened during Bush's presidency. Government agencies prevented some terrorist plans. In 2003 the FBI discovered a plot to blow up the Brooklyn Bridge in New York City. In 2006 the FBI arrested seven men for a plot to blow up Chicago's Willis Tower.

The president believed he had protected the nation. According to Bush, the Patriot Act and other new laws helped the government catch terrorists. Many Americans agree. But some say the policies hurt Americans' freedoms without preventing terrorist attacks.

In 2008 the US Supreme Court made a ruling about prisoners at Guantanamo Bay. It said that people held at the prison had the right to argue in court that they were illegally held. The Bush administration eventually released or transferred more than 500 people from the prison.

In early 2009, Bush prepared to leave office. The war in Afghanistan continued. Troops captured or killed many

Another Battle

In March 2003, the United States sent troops to invade the country of Iraq. Iraqi dictator Saddam Hussein was thought to possess very destructive weapons and have links to al-Qaeda. US-led forces overthrew Hussein's government within weeks. Troops captured Hussein in December 2003. And a new Iraqi government took over in June 2004. But it faced strong resistance.

Later in 2004, an investigation found no evidence that Hussein had been connected to al-Qaeda. Another stated there was not evidence that Hussein had possessed advanced weapons. The reports made many people wonder why the United States had gone to Iraq. US troops stayed in Iraq until December 2011.

A coalition military officer says farewell to his replacement commander. The coalition officially ended the war in Afghanistan in December 2014.

people involved with terrorist groups. But the war was lasting much longer than many people expected. In 2010 it became the longest war in US history. Thousands of Americans died in the war.

The war remains controversial. Some people support the government's actions. They believe it was necessary to act quickly after the September 11 attacks. Others believe the Bush administration should have planned the invasion more carefully. A better plan might have led to a shorter war.

On January 15, 2009, shortly before leaving office, Bush delivered a speech to the American public. "As the years passed, most Americans were able to return to life much as it had been before 9/11," he said. "But I never did." September 11, 2001, defined Bush's presidency. And Bush's response to the September 11 attacks continues to shape the role the US government has in the lives of Americans and in countries around the world.

FURTHER EVIDENCE

Chapter Four describes how the United States changed after September 11. What is one of the main points of the chapter? What evidence is included to support this point? Read the article at the website below. Find one piece of evidence to support the main point of the chapter.

September 11 to Now

mycorelibrary.com/george-w.-bush

IMPORTANT DATES

Sept. 11, 2001

Hijackers crash planes into both World Trade Center towers, the Pentagon, and a field in Virginia.

Sept. 14, 2001

George W. Bush tours Ground Zero, where the World Trade Center once stood, in New York City.

Sept. 20, 2001

In a speech to the nation, Bush announces a war on terror.

Oct. 26, 2001

The president signs the Patriot Act into law.

Nov. 25, 2002

Bush signs a bill that creates the Department of Homeland Security.

Mar. 20, 2003

US troops invade Iraq.

Sept. 22, 2001

Bush signs an act of Congress that creates the September 11 Victim Compensation Fund.

Sept. 27, 2001

Bush announces new air-safety measures.

Oct. 7, 2001

Bush announces the beginning of Operation Enduring Freedom.

Oct. 9, 2004

The new Afghan government holds its first presidential election.

Jan. 15, 2009

Bush gives a farewell address.

May 2, 2011

US navy commandos in Pakistan find and kill Osama bin Laden.

STOP AND THINK

Why Do I Care?

The September 11 attacks happened more than a decade ago. How do these attacks affect Americans today? Think about how Americans still remember what happened on September 11, 2001. How did this event change the United States?

Tell the Tale

Chapter Two of this book discusses Bush's visit to New York after the terrorist attacks. Imagine you are making a similar journey. Write 200 words about what you see. What people do you meet? What do you see and hear?

Surprise Me

Chapter Three gives facts about Afghanistan. What two or three facts about Afghanistan did you find most surprising? Write a few sentences about each fact. Why did you find each fact surprising?

Take a Stand

Bush believed nations that hid terrorists should be punished. This belief caused him to support a war in Afghanistan. Do you agree with Bush? Based on this, was war the right decision? Why or why not?

GLOSSARY

administration
a group of government officials working for a president

bioterrorism
using toxic substances as weapons

coalition
a group of people or nations working together for a common cause

dictator
a ruler with total power over a country

hijacker
someone who forcefully takes control of a vehicle

militant
involved in fighting or warfare

motorcade
a line of vehicles that escorts a person from one place to another

surveillance
continual observation in order to gather information

terrorist
someone who uses violence to threaten or scare others

waterboarding
repeatedly forcing water into a person's mouth and nose

LEARN MORE

Books

Benoit, Peter. *September 11: We Will Never Forget*. New York: Scholastic, 2012.

Brown, Don. *America Is Under Attack: The Day the Towers Fell*. New York: Roaring Brook, 2014.

Gormley, Beatrice. *President George W. Bush: Our Forty-Third President*. New York: Aladdin, 2005.

Websites

To learn more about Presidential Perspectives, visit **booklinks.abdopublishing.com**. These links are routinely monitored and updated to provide the most current information available.

Visit **mycorelibrary.com** for free additional tools for teachers and students.

INDEX

ABOUT THE AUTHOR

Emily O'Keefe is a writer, editor, and teacher. She is the author of several books for young people. Her interests include history, literature, and travel. O'Keefe lives in Chicago, Illinois, with her cat, Chloe.